101
BUSINESS
TIPS

KAREN TAYLOR

101 Business Tips for Independent Business Owners
First edition published 2021
©Copyright Karen Taylor

Published by Dr Tony Henshall
Cheshire
UK

https://www.karenyourbusinessmentor.com

Book Mentoring and Editing by Siân-Elin Flint-Freel
Author photograph by Senem Peace Photography

Paperback ISBN 978-1-8384808-2-0

This book is dedicated to independent business owners everywhere. Working for yourself is not an easy option but it's one you will never regret. Remember, we are the backbone of the economy. Get out there and prosper!

FOREWORD

My Facebook group was formed for the purpose of supporting the people who attend my business networking events in and around Cheshire. I try to make the content as interesting and varied as possible and knew that if Karen gave us simple business tips each week it would be a useful addition.

Many of us in the group are not naturally business-minded. There are many talented creatives and also several people who have started businesses after being employed for many years. We needed to learn how to make our new ventures profitable.

Fortunately, Karen was up for the challenge and agreed to give us simple yet effective tips every Monday. Her column soon became very popular. Many people said they looked out for the tip before they started the week and used it as a motivating call to action for that day. Even those who ran successful businesses with good strategies in place enjoyed the weekly reminders and commented in approval.

After 101 weeks of solid advice, it was obvious these tips needed to be transferred into a valuable pocket guide and this is what Karen has done.

What I especially love about this book is the way Karen has included quotes from those endorsing her advice and showing how they make a real difference.

This is a timeless book of tips which will serve you well. Karen's approach is easy to follow and makes perfect sense. I know you will enjoy dipping in and out of the pages as much as I did.

Sue France

Creative Connecting in Cheshire

INTRODUCTION

I never thought I would write a book...it definitely wasn't on my bucket list!

In November 2018 I started writing business tips for a Facebook group called 'Sue France Creative Connecting in Cheshire'. I posted one tip a week to see how it went. It went well; there was lots of interest and comments. So I decided I would write 52, one for each week of the year. With a few weeks off for holidays and Christmas, 52 Business Tips took me to the beginning of 2020. We all know what happened next – a global pandemic!

I had more business tips in my head, so I continued to write my business tips and post them once a week, eventually stopping in February 2021 when I had written 101.

This book is a culmination of those business tips plus comments business owners have made about the tip and how it works for them.

You might be puzzled by the order of the business tips. The order hasn't been changed. It is exactly the same order as I wrote them. I've kept them that way. They are random. But you will notice some tips look grouped together, as this is just how they flowed out of my head!

The book can be read start to finish, Business Tip no. 1 to no. 101, or you can just delve in. Open the book and read what you see, take time to digest the tip, think about you and your business.

★ Does the tip resonate with you?
★ Can you use it?
★ Can you adapt it?

I've even jotted down some quick wins that you can act on straight away.

Everything I do as a Business Mentor is about my clients: small independent (usually female) business owners. This book is for them and about them!

BUSINESS TIP NO. 1

Do what you love

This is the first business tip because it's the most important.

If you are not doing what you love – why not? This is your chance to show the world your 'thing' in life and what you are most passionate about. If you don't love what you do, then you might as well go and work for somebody else because it's much easier!!!

So true - if you love it, it shows. It's not a job, it's a passion.

Julie Elder

Totally agree with this! I'm finally loving my job. Feel like it's more of a hobby because I get so much enjoyment out of it. Almost feels wrong!!

Anna Van Der Feltz

Totally what the first tip should be. You spend so much of your life in work, you have to love it otherwise find something else to do.

Sian Pelleschi

BUSINESS TIP NO. 2

Be yourself

This is the second most important tip for small business owners following on from tip no. 1 'Do what you love'.

'Be Yourself' – because why not! It's so much easier in life. You don't have to be anyone else or pretend to be anything else when you work for yourself. Not everybody will be your cup of tea or you theirs and that's perfectly fine.

Stay true to who you are, don't put on a posh telephone voice, as people prefer people who keep it real. Times are changing, you can still be professional no matter what you wear and how you sound. If anyone tries to put you off aiming high or says you can't do something, then use that as fuel to your fire to push you. Don't let anyone put you off. Go for it.

Karen Lee

BUSINESS TIP NO. 3

Be consistent

Success comes from being consistent. People need to recognise you at a glance and know it's you and your business.

Have you started to recognise these business tips because they all look the same and therefore you spot them and know what they are?

QUICK WIN

Go to one of your social media pages. Have a look at a few of your posts and try to view it as someone from the outside looking in.

At a quick glance, are your posts consistent?

BUSINESS TIP NO. 4

Niche your business

Does your business have a niche? Do you know what it is?
Niching is all about narrowing down your business and being very specific about who you are and what you do.

These days, the smaller the niche (or micro-niche) the better. Google particularly loves small niche businesses and it is more likely to find your business in a search than if you are very general.

That's why you now see businesses such as yoga for babies in Manchester, gifts made from dog's paw prints in Cheshire, etc.

Being niche means I can stay focused on what I love, what I want to sell and be able to share feeling fabulous, all while staying true to myself. I have a very niche business. Because of this, people know exactly that they are in the right place for them and become customers rather than lost browsers. Being niche doesn't restrict your customer base. In fact, being niche can increase it.

Donna Law

BUSINESS TIP NO. 5

Be visible

Get out there and be seen. Whether it's online or in person. People soon forget a business that's hiding away. You need to keep popping up, it reminds people who you are and what you do!

It's really important to remember that the 'social' part of social media is key. I try to post regularly and to keep the posts spontaneous and authentic so that people build up a relationship and trust me. In the future, that trust may convert to a sale.

Sam Baguley

BUSINESS TIP NO. 6

Keep it simple

Says it all. If you are not clear and simple in everything you do in your business then people just won't get it!

The more you can keep it simple, the more your clients/customers will get it and therefore the more business you will get.

Simples!

I so resonate with this hence my business name, Simply Solved. I'm a firm believer in keeping things nice and straightforward. I like to provide regular work updates for my clients so that they are clear where their tasks are up to at any given time.

Debbie Harvey

BUSINESS TIP NO. 7

Know your turnover,

gross profit & net profit

If you only know 3 numbers in your business, make it these 3! If you don't know these numbers each month, then you don't know your business.

In simple terms they are:
- ★ Turnover (or Revenue or Total Sales) – the total amount coming into your business
- ★ Gross Profit – turnover minus the costs of making and selling your products or services
- ★ Net Profit (or bottom line or actual profit) – Gross Profit minus everything it costs to run your business or the final amount you have left.

QUICK WIN

If you don't regularly know these 3 numbers, then spend some time working them out for the last month.

BUSINESS TIP NO. 8

Have 12-month goals

At the start of each new year most small business owners' thoughts turn to setting goals. I like to do mine in September as it feels more like a better time to do it. It doesn't matter when you set goals for your business, the most important thing is that you set them!

Goals are very important, they help us to keep our business moving and to grow. And we need to keep moving and growing. If we don't, things WILL happen around us which could affect our business and which may not necessarily be for the best. Just think of the troubles the high street retailers are in!

QUICK WIN

If you haven't got any goals for your business, think about where you want your business to be in 12 months' time. How do you want it to look, to sound like, to feel like?

BUSINESS TIP NO. 9

Have SMART goals

Most small businesses only need goals for 12 months otherwise they are too far away. Things can change a lot even within 12 months.

I love SMART (Specific, Measurable, Achievable, Realistic, Timebound) goals because they work!

A lot of small business owners will write a goal that says: 'I want to make more money' or 'I want to sell more products', which doesn't actually say anything.

But rewritten as 'In my beauty business I want to increase my turnover by 10% to x amount by the end of the year'. It says much more, has numbers in it you can measure and a date by which to reach it.

QUICK WIN

Practice by writing your last goal in a sentence the SMART way.

BUSINESS TIP NO. 10

Plot your turnover on a graph

This topic came up during one of my Accountability Groups. It is important that you are tracking the numbers in your business and a good way of doing this is to plot your turnover on a graph.

In Microsoft Excel (or something similar), create a table and record your turnover for each month, then create a line graph from these numbers. You can then add each year onto the graph. If the idea of spreadsheets fills you with dread, ask for some help from your accountant or someone who loves them!

It is simple but it will give you a lot of information about your business. It will show how you are growing over the years but mainly it shows the peaks and troughs in your year. Knowing this information means that you can anticipate when the quieter times will be in your year and therefore plan accordingly.

Here's an example of turnover plotted over 3 years.

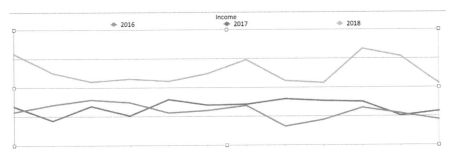

Before working with Karen I never saw the importance of tracking figures. I was aware of them but never really looked at them in a way that would help my business. By tracking my revenue and turnover on a graph it was easy to see how my business was progressing each month AND more importantly I was able to compare each month. This made it easier to forecast my turnover for the end of the year and I could see progression in my business year on year.

Julie Elder

BUSINESS TIP NO. 11

Record your social media numbers each month

This tip is another one about knowing the numbers in your business and therefore understanding more about your business.

Each month write down the number of followers/likes for each of your social media platforms. If you start at the beginning of the year, then at the end of the year you can look back and see how far you have come. Reward yourself and give yourself a pat on the back!

If you are not writing these numbers down then at the end of the year you won't have a clue how many more followers/likes you now have.

The increase in these numbers shows the growth and spread of people who know you and your business. These people choose to see your social media posts and therefore reflect the growth in your business.

QUICK WIN

If you are not doing this...start now!

BUSINESS TIP NO. 12

Make sure you have

Terms & Conditions

You'd be surprised at how many small businesses don't have 'Terms & Conditions'. I send all my new clients a copy of my T&C's document (and my GDPR policy!). If unfortunately something does go wrong, then you have your document to refer to.

There are lots of examples on the internet of what a terms & conditions document should look like. If you haven't got one, find one you like and adapt it for your business.

Also make sure it's added as a link to your website.

BUSINESS TIP NO. 13

Register your business on

Google My Business

Obviously the biggest search engine in the world is important to all small businesses, as we all want our business to appear in the search results when a potential customer wants a service or product.

Two of the main things Google is looking for from a small business are:
1. Are you real (!)?
2. Are you active?

Registering your business on Google Business shows you are real and also lets you add your address, opening hours, location, website, etc. so that your details display when your business is found.

Google My Business also has lots of insights (statistics) showing how people search for your business, where the search comes from, what they do when they find you, etc. Fascinating stuff!!!

QUICK WIN

If you are not registered on 'Google My Business', then you should be. It takes 5 minutes to set it up. Do it now!

BUSINESS TIP NO. 14

Add a post to Google My Business each week

In 'Business Tip No. 13' I said that two of the main things Google is looking for from a small business are:
1. Are you real (!)?
2. Are you active?

Adding a post to Google My Business shows you are alive and active! The more Google knows we are real and active, the more it likes us and therefore the more it will show our business (and higher up) in the search results.

Unfortunately the posts only last 7 days, so I would only add 1 post, then after 7 days when it has expired, add another one.

QUICK WIN

Use your last social media post and add it to 'Google My Business'

BUSINESS TIP NO. 15

*Add your logo on all images
and use your branding
colours and fonts*

This is so important for all your social media images. People need to recognise your business straight away. So add your logo and use your branding colours and fonts.

If you don't know how to do this, have a look at 'Canva', a fantastic free tool for social media images.

BUSINESS TIP NO. 16

Don't use acronyms, jargon or technical words

This is when you are describing your business, either in writing (e.g. on your website) or speaking to someone else.

Make sure you can describe your business in clear, simple words that anybody can understand, even a child.

It sounds easy but I am always surprised, particularly at networking meetings, how some people describe their business. They use acronyms, jargon or technical words that mean lots to them and their industry/ profession but I'm not clear what their business is or does!! Please don't be this person.

Very true. Think in terms of the language that your audience will be familiar with. A good example of this is: electricians will refer to a consumer unit which most of us call a fuse box.

Judith Todd

This is sound advice. People always presume that just because they use a word everyday that everyone else knows what it means. If it's a word used in your industry and not theirs, just explain.

Sue France

BUSINESS TIP NO. 17

It's called social media

- be sociable

I often say this to my clients and it's obvious when you think about it, but the more you are sociable on social media the more other people will be sociable with you!

Social media is a very important (and free) marketing tool for small businesses, so make the most of it and cultivate (virtual) relationships.

You never know where it might lead!

QUICK WIN

Next time you are scrolling through social media, stop and make a conscience effort to interact with a post.

BUSINESS TIP NO. 18

Spend 1-2 hours a week

working ON your business

Do you spend time working ON your business to plan, organise, develop and move your business forward?

All small business owners are very busy running the business as we have to be a jack of all trades. But spending time working on your business will pay off and just 1–2 hours a week is all you need.

The trick is to block out the time in your diary, stick to the time, get out your to–do list and tick the items of your list. Or use it as thinking time for where you want your business to go.

Spend 1–2 hours a week to move your business forward and it will pay off.

Unique Selling Point (USP) is very important to a small business as:

QUICK WIN

When is the quietest time in your week? It may be Monday morning, Wednesday lunchtime or Friday afternoon? Now block out 2 hours next week in that slot to work ON your business and stick to it.

BUSINESS TIP NO. 19

Know your USP - why you?

- ★ It makes you stand out
- ★ It sets you apart from the rest
- ★ It differentiates you

We need it because:
- ★ We all have competition
- ★ It makes people buy from us
- ★ No two businesses are the same (even if they look the same they won't be because we all have different backgrounds, skills and knowledge)
- ★ People buy from people!!

So, make sure you know your USP!

Having a USP works! People buy from people. Under-promise and over-achieve always. Be WYSIWYG (what you see is what you get) and be consistent in your voice.

Debby Marcy

BUSINESS TIP NO. 20

Know your Super Customers

A lot of business coaches/mentors talk about your 'Ideal Client/Customer'. I don't like this term as it feels like I've made up this ideal client and now I've got to go out and find them. It's like looking for a needle in a haystack!!!

Super Customer is different, as its based on the best customers you already have. Obviously the more super customers we can attract the better for us and our business.

To find your Super Customer or Client: write down the names of your top clients & their characteristics e.g. male or female, age, type of business (if you work B2B), age of business, their personality, etc.

The characteristics you choose could be different to this, choose what works for your business. Analyse what you see and you will find similar characteristics between your top clients. These are your Super Customers.
This works – Super Customers are based on real people.

Although I use the term 'ideal client', this is exactly what I've done to develop my customer profiles. I still tweak my ideal client/ super customer profile as things occur to me or my business changes.

Louise Barson

BUSINESS TIP NO. 21

Know your pitch in one paragraph

The last two Business Tips have been about your USP and your Super Customer. An easy way to write yourself a pitch which you can use to describe your business either at networking events or to family and friends is to write 3 sentences...

★ 1st sentence – Describe your business in easy, simple terms (which we covered in Business Tip no. 16)

★ 2nd sentence – Explain your USP

★ 3rd sentence – Characterise/depict/outline your Super Customers

Merge the 3 sentences together and you have a pitch, which is short, concise and with no rambling!

BUSINESS TIP NO. 22

Spend a lot more time retaining customers than trying to get new ones!

Apparently it can be up to 6/7 times harder to get a new customer than to retain the customers you've already got or get past customers to come back.

Therefore, by that theory, we should be spending a lot more time and effort in retaining existing customers than trying to get new ones. Which is a much better idea, as lets face it, getting new customers is hard!

I am always amazed at the amount of effort some people put into attracting new customers, totally disregarding the loyal regulars. My mother and stepfather used to visit a cafe in San Pedro for many years. Each time they were welcomed back like long lost friends, hugged and given a good table. It wasn't the cheapest or the best of the many restaurants there, but the welcome they gave ensured that my family always returned and continued to recommend it to their friends.

Sue France

BUSINESS TIP NO. 23

Ask all customers for reviews/recommendations

Customer reviews or recommendations are worth their weight in gold. The power of what somebody else says about you and your business cannot be underestimated.

Research shows that customer reviews are nearly 12 times more trusted than descriptions which come from the business itself.

So make sure you collect as many as you can and use them to your advantage on your website and social media.

QUICK WIN

Who did you last work with? Ask them for a review NOW!

BUSINESS TIP NO. 24

Don't say WE if there is only

you in your business

This is a particular bug bear of mine!

Why put 'WE' on your website, your blogs or in social media posts, when there is only you in your business?

There is nothing wrong with saying it's me, I do everything and I'm proud of running my small business on my own.

I really need to get out of this habit. It was drummed into me when I started my business that you shouldn't allow anyone to think it is only you! So I always say we and feel really silly.

Alison Calder

BUSINESS TIP NO. 25

Spend money in local small businesses and they will support you back

As a small business owner, I am big on supporting other small businesses as much as I can. If we support our local small businesses then the money stays in the local economy, supporting the local community.

If you spend your money in big corporate businesses, the money and profits definitely go out of the local economy. Who knows where it is going???

If we all encourage each other to support local small businesses, then it will come round and we will get supported back! Fantastic!

QUICK WIN

Next time you are popping out to the shops or ordering online, think...can I buy this at a small independent business?

BUSINESS TIP NO. 26

Find networking groups that you like and work for you and stick with them

When I worked in the corporate world, I didn't even know that networking groups even existed! Now I realise there are tons of them and you could go to one every day of the week.

One thing I have learned is that they are all different. When I first started working for myself I tried lots of different ones and soon realised which I liked and which worked for me. Once you find the right networks, stick with them, as the more you go to the same ones, the more you get to know people and build relationships.

Now I stick to just three different ones that I like and which work for me!

Absolutely! After going to lots of different networking groups, I too have found the ones I really like.

Natasha Diskin

BUSINESS TIP NO. 27

Ignore what everybody else is doing, stick to your guns and what's right for you

It's very easy, particularly with social media, to think that everybody is doing absolutely fantastic and so much better than you. Very rarely do people post bad things on social media or photos of their beans on toast lunch!!

There is a lot of smoke and mirrors going on. So please don't get caught with comparison syndrome. If you feel this is happening to you, put on your blinkers and stick to your guns for what's right for you and your business.

Totally agree — it's so easy to get sucked into believing everyone else is having the most perfect time!

Sian Pelleschi

Used to tell my students that the others might be wrong!!

Val Pallister

BUSINESS TIP NO. 28

If you are having a bad day/week/month look at the bigger picture and usually it's all ok

We can all have a bad day or week or even month, particularly if you work on your own. It can be difficult to keep motivated and moving forward with your business.

But a bad day/week/month does not make a bad business. Step back and look at the whole picture. Look at your sales/turnover/profit for the past 6 months or year. How does this look?

No business has the same amount of sales every month. Look over the past year and if your monthly average is what you are aiming for, then you are fine.

Give yourself a pat on the back, you are doing great!!!

BUSINESS TIP NO. 29

Accountability keeps you motivated and moving your business along

I love accountability for keeping motivated and getting stuff done because simply – it works!

The fact that somebody is going to ask you about something makes you do it!! That's it!

If you haven't got accountability for your business, then I recommend you get some. It can be from meeting a like–minded business owner in a coffee shop once a month to being part of a mastermind group.

I run monthly 1–1 accountability sessions and accountability groups for up to 5 female business owners. If you are interested in either, get in touch.

Accountability is invaluable for me as a solo business owner. Regular sessions show me what I'm doing right, what I could do better, and what I'm not doing effectively — all in a constructive and positive way.

Sam Baguley

BUSINESS TIP NO. 30

Don't be frightened of

asking for deposits

A lot of clients I talk to don't like asking for money, never mind asking for a deposit! Why not? We are not a charity, we don't do this as a hobby, we need money to run our businesses and to live.

The problem with not asking for a deposit is that people don't necessary think it is serious and feel ok to cancel and mess you about. If they pay a deposit then you know they are committing and definitely want your offering.

Just set yourself a process, put it in your 'terms & conditions', send them an invoice (or however you take payments) and let them know the booking is confirmed once the deposit is paid.

Actually the best way is to get paid is in full, upfront! Then you have your money before you exchange your product or service. If you have a retail business or use a booking app, this is easy to do. Or if you organise events or workshops, use something like Eventbrite.

People are getting more and more used to paying upfront. Make it easy for yourself!

Well said! I now request money up front due to businesses failing to pay or constantly chasing payment being an absolutely pain. What a hassle I have had. I could write a book!

Kerry Louise Burgess

Because of your encouragement, I now get new clients to pay for their first session upfront and nobody has ever questioned it!

Zoë Oughton

If you feel awkward about asking for money, it's so much easier to ask for it up front than chasing after you have provided the service anyway
I honestly think people rarely question it for most services.

Jemma Munford

QUICK WIN

For your next client, ask for a deposit.

BUSINESS TIP NO. 31

Take a small step every day to move your business forward

This tip really works and it doesn't have to be something big that takes a lot of time. Just think – 'Today what am I going to move my business forward'.

So it could be: sending a message to someone you've been meaning to contact, creating an image in Canva or writing an interesting social media post.

Anything that takes you a few minutes and remember, small things all add up!!!

QUICK WIN

What will be your step today to move your business forward?

BUSINESS TIP NO. 32

Only 20% of social media posts should be selling

Lets face it, social media is addictive but it can be dull! Nobody wants to see a business constantly pushing obvious selling posts in your face. It doesn't make people buy – in fact, it pushes them away!

Social media is all about building followers of your business and creating relationships with these followers. Then hopefully they will get to 'know, like and trust' you to become a customer or client.

The best way is to share interesting posts relevant to you and your business but not obvious selling posts.

Examples are:
★ what you are doing in your day
★ who you are meeting
★ recommendations
★ sharing blogs
★ quotes, etc.

So think, 80% interesting posts, 20% promoting my products/services. I find pictures of my no.1 employee, 'Bob the dog' always go down well!!!

Only use the social media platforms where your customers are

Nobody has the time or energy to post and be active on every social media platform. You just end up spreading yourself too thinly and not doing anything well, trying to attract followers that are never going to be interested.

So find out where your followers, potential clients and current clients hang out, stick to those social media platforms and do it well. Two or three platforms is enough.

There is a theory that says you should spend 90% of your time on the social media platforms which work for you and only 10% of your time on the others, keeping a vague presence. Sounds good to me!

QUICK WIN

List the top two platforms where your ideal client/customers spend most of their time.

BUSINESS TIP NO. 34

Promote your business in

Facebook groups

Facebook groups are great for small businesses, as we get to promote our business for free to more (hopefully interested) people.

I'm not an expert on Facebook but I know that it doesn't like business pages (as it wants us to pay) and is putting a lot more effort into groups. It wants groups to be the cornerstone of Facebook and the main reason why we use it.

Facebook groups are going to become more important to small business owners in the future, so let's use them to build relationships and get free advertising!

QUICK WIN

Promote your business in a Facebook group today!

BUSINESS TIP NO. 35

Know your

breakeven point

Do you know the breakeven point for your business? If not, you should do!

It's the point where the total sales and the total expenses are the same, therefore anything after this point is profit. And we all love profit!!

It can also be the number of products/services you need to sell to cover your costs.

A simple way to calculate your breakeven point is:

$$fixed\ costs \div (price - variable\ costs) = breakeven\ point$$

So if my fixed costs (rent, insurance, heating, etc.) cost £1000 a month, and I sell my product/service at £100 and it costs £10 to produce (variable cost)

$$1000 \div (100 - 10) = 11.1$$

Breakeven point is 11.1, so I need to sell 12 of my product/service before I start to make a profit.

If you would like any help calculating your breakeven point, just ask.

BUSINESS TIP NO. 36

Employ intelligent, motivated people

I first heard this from Sir Gerry Robinson who used to be the head of Granada TV, amongst other roles, and has had various TV shows as a business troubleshooter. He says when employing people the key is to choose intelligent, motivated people as anything else you can teach them.

It sounds too simple but if you think about it...

BUSINESS TIP NO. 37

Don't hide your prices

In the UK we like to know how much things cost. Shops display prices in their windows, online commerce websites always show their prices, etc.

Do you have a website or post on social media but are not telling people how much your products or services cost?

If we can't see a price we don't know if it's £100 or £1000 and if we can't see a price we all automatically assume we can't afford it!

By displaying your prices, people who can afford your product or service will read on. It will also stop pointless enquiries from people who cannot afford your products/services and are never going to buy form you.

Always display your prices and be open and transparent.

I agree with this 100%. When I walk into a designer shop where no prices are displayed I remember the old adage "If you have to ask you can't afford it". A customer will often feel too embarrassed and just walk out again. I believe a lot of small business owners fall into the trap of not advertising prices because they make individual items which are dearer than mass produced and they think if they make the prices visible straight away, it will put people off. I think it's the very opposite. People expect to pay more for unique and handmade.

In these days of instant purchases, if people have to search for your prices, they just move on.

Sue France

BUSINESS TIP NO. 38

Look after the pennies &

the pounds will look

after themselves

I'm sure you have probably heard this one before; it's an old english proverb relating to looking after your money.

Pennies aren't worth a lot these days but I think the sentiment still applies today in business. If you look after your pennies, they become pounds. And you could say if you look after the pounds, they become hundreds of pounds and then thousands of pounds. In other words, know exactly where all the pennies are in your business.

For instance: If you are paying just £10 a month for something, this is £120 a year. Obvious I know but do you really want be be spending £120 a year on it?

QUICK WIN

Have a scan down your last bank statement and look at your direct debits. Are you paying for something you no longer need?

BUSINESS TIP NO. 39

Raise your prices every year

Everything else goes up every year, so why aren't you raising your prices every year?

Nobody likes to raise their prices because we always think we are going to lose customer/clients. In practice, what actually happens is, you might lose some customers but the extra money you make from your increased prices more than makes up for the lost customers.

And if you do lose any customers, they tend to be the ones you don't want, the headaches, because they were only buying on price and not for the extra values you give!!
Try it and see...

You're right, it's always a challenge and I never do it. But life's bills do rise every year - from electric to provisions.

Nicky Abell–Francis

That's very true, Karen. The satisfaction of working with people who are aware of the extra value you're giving is worth taking that risk. It also shows the respect to what you do too, doesn't it?

Senem Peace

BUSINESS TIP NO. 40

Support each other online

As small business owners, we can help each other in lots of ways. One great way is to support each other online.

It doesn't matter which social media platform you prefer, start by following other small business owners' pages. Then when you see their posts, 'like, comment or share' their posts.

When you do this, it automatically increases their visibility and more people they don't know will see their posts.

It all helps!

QUICK WIN

Next time you are scrolling through social media, make a point of searching around and liking 3 business pages which attract you.

BUSINESS TIP NO. 41

Networking is about getting to know people & building relationships

We've all been to networking meetings where people push their business cards in your face and if they are not interested in your business they move on and work the room!

Does this work? NO!

We like to get to know people, we like to trust them and we all like people like us!

So if you go to a networking event thinking about selling, then it's not going to work but if you go to meet new people, get to know them and build a relationship. Then it will work.

People buy from people and people buy from people they know, like and trust.

Totally agree with this, Karen. My intent is always to listen and learn. People see through others only at an event to push their own agenda.

Michelle Mullany

BUSINESS TIP NO. 42

Networking is all about planting seeds

When you go to a networking event the chances of somebody wanting what you are offering at exactly that time is going to be very slim.

All you are doing is planting seeds... building relationships, so people get to know, like and trust you. When in 6 months, 12 months' time or even longer and when they are interested in what you are offering, then they will remember you.

Or if they know somebody else who might be interested in your offering and then they remember and recommend you. How cool is that when people are recommending you to people you have never even met!

Planting seeds...it takes time but it will pay off.

I run networking events and they are all about planting seeds, making new connections to create strong working relationships, which in return grows your business.

Tricia Peters

BUSINESS TIP NO. 43

Don't worry if your turnover is like a rollercoaster

No business takes the same turnover each month. Some months we will take more and some months we will take less. This fluctuation is normal.

This could be due to summer holidays, Christmas and other factors. The thing is not to worry and do not to panic if you have a quiet month.

Look back, see the bigger picture, know which are the busier months.

Think this is normal, my turnover is a rollercoaster and what comes down must go up!!!

Believe in yourself, you can do this!

BUSINESS TIP NO. 44

Ask NEW clients/customers

to pay upfront

Sometimes I think as female business owners we can be very trusting, particularly if you have a service business. We say 'It's ok, you can pay later', or 'Pay afterwards'.

I think this is fine if it's somebody you know or if you've already worked with them and you feel you can trust them. But what if it's a new customer/client, somebody you don't know, and you might not even have met them?

Ask them to pay when they book. You will find that nobody complains. In fact, you could always ask people to pay upfront every time they book with you. If you still feel uneasy asking for payments upfront – you can always ask for a deposit or offer a refund if not entirely satisfied.

If you think about it, a lot of times we are asked to pay for something before we have received it, like in retail or through online booking systems. It is becoming more and more the normal thing to do, so why should your small business be different?

This resonates and is a great tip for me to read...I am very trusting but this can get equally annoying when clients ask can they pay by bank transfer which is what I offer...but then on occasions money hasn't gone through and can be 2 days or more!!

I mean, when you get your hair done you don't make the hairdresser wait or pay later for your food shopping or paying for a meal in a restaurant in 2/3 days!!!!

Julie Widdowson

I always ask for payment up front for new clients. I was too trusting when I started my business and a couple of people took advantage of that, but not any more!

Sally Smith

BUSINESS TIP NO. 45

People buy from people

This might be a cliche but it's so true! You might buy from somebody once because you need what they are offering but what makes you buy from them again?

Most of the time it will be something to do with the business/person you interacted with. Think about what makes you buy from somebody over and over again?

The more we buy from a particular business the more it will be because of a person or experience we have received. It will make us come back.

As small business owners we can excel on this, give the personal touch, go the extra mile and look after our Super Customers.

This is good because people like to buy from real people not a faceless business!

BUSINESS TIP NO. 46

You are your business

If there is just you in your business or if you are a business owner with employees, either way 'You are the business'. The business is YOU!

Because if it's your business, you set the tone, the culture and you make all the important decisions.

So exploit this fact, sell you, talk about you, promote yourself! Remember Business Tip No. 45: 'People buy from people'!

Be personable. The more we are personable the more people will buy from us.

BUSINESS TIP NO. 47

Get out & meet people

When I was young my mother used to say 'Boyfriends don't come knocking'!! What she meant was, if I wanted a boyfriend, they don't come knocking at the door (well not for me!), you have to go out and meet one.

And I soon realised that if you want anything in life, be it a boyfriend, friend, work or business, then you have to go out into the big, scary world and find what you're looking for – it won't come knocking on your door!

So it's the same in business. You can't just sit in a safe, comfy place, you have to put yourself out there. Make that phone call, go to the networking meeting, send the email...talk to people, meet people and like I always say... you never know where it might lead!

BUSINESS TIP NO. 48

Look for collaborations

Aristotle said: 'The whole is greater than the sum of its parts'. It means that together we are greater than the separate parts on their own. Or 1+1 doesn't equal 2 but something far more...

Why collaborations are good for small business owners:
- ★ You can do bigger projects together that you wouldn't even consider or couldn't do on your own
- ★ You are not working on your own (after many years out of the corporate world, I still miss working in a team)
- ★ You both bring different skills, knowledge and experience
- ★ You automatically get more followers/existing clients
- ★ You share the highs and the lows
- ★ You are equal
- ★ You can open doors for each other. With the people they know and the people you know

It's a 'win–win' situation. Start looking for suitable collaborations to work with. It might work out, it might not but you never know unless you try.

I've learnt that it's important to find collaborators within a similar field and with the same business/work/lifestyle ethic as you.

Natasha Diskin

BUSINESS TIP NO. 49

Plan for the dips in your

rollercoaster

Remember Business Tip No. 43 – 'Don't worry if your turnover is like a rollercoaster'? Once you have realised that this is normal, you will start to notice when the high turnover months are and when the low turnover months are.

You may also start to see a pattern, particularly after a few years, that the high and the low months appear in the same places. For instance, I now know that my 'low' months every year are August and December.

Once you have this knowledge you can then plan to do something about it, so that next time the low months maybe aren't too bad.

For example: last August I had an offer on one of my packages and it worked well, I got some bookings that I wouldn't have had and made more money than the August the year before.

So try something different for your 'low' months and see what happens...

BUSINESS TIP NO. 50

Break your goals down

into milestones

At the start of a new year, it's traditional for small business owners to think about their business, where they would like it to go in the next year, set some goals and create a plan of how to get there.

I'm not a huge fan of big, cumbersome business pans that people write and mainly stick in a drawer or file away and never look at again. But I am a strong believer that small business owners do need goals and plans that work for them, that they love and use to grow their business.

I've written a couple of Business Tips already around goals (Business Tips no. 8 & 9), so the next few Business Tips will be around planning.

Once you have a goal for the next 12 months, it can seem big and daunting. The tip here is to break it down into smaller milestones. I find 4 in a year – one every quarter usually work well for me and my clients. e.g. Jan – Mar, Apr – Jun, Jul – Sep, Oct – Dec

Each milestone should also be written in the SMART format. They must be Specific, Measurable, Achievable, Relevant, and Timebound.

Then you can take the first milestone and start your planning...

BUSINESS TIP NO. 51

Have a plan

This may seen obvious but I am always surprised by how many business owners don't have a plan. They just get 'stuck in' and work very hard all year and don't seem to get very far. They work hard and hope to achieve their goal, but somehow it just doesn't happen.

Why do you need a plan?

Your plan is the steps that you will need to take so that you will achieve your goal. Quite simply, without a plan you will never reach your goal because you won't know how you are going to get there and you won't know when you have arrived.

So you need a goal (Business Tip No. 8) and you need a plan which explains how you are going to get to that goal.

> Spend time creating a goal and a plan for what you want for your business and it will pay off.

BUSINESS TIP NO. 52

Break down your plan into small tasks

There are lots of ways to create a plan for your milestone. The easiest way I recommend is:

1. Start BIG – write down all the big tasks that you need to do which will get you to your milestone
2. Break down the big tasks into smaller tasks
3. Break down the small tasks into even smaller tasks
4. Keep breaking down the tasks until you get to tasks small enough for your to–do list.

If you struggle to get going with the big tasks, I find it helps to think of them under 3 categories:

★ What are you going to do for existing clients to get to your milestone?
★ What are you going to do for new clients to get to your milestone?
★ Other activities which will help you get to your milestone, e.g. website, flyers, social media, etc.

BUSINESS TIP NO. 53

Use sticky notes

for planning

In tip no. 52 I explained a process for creating a plan involving breaking down tasks into small tasks. A good way to do this is by using sticky notes.

Write each individual task on a sticky note. Then it's easier to stick them on a big piece of paper, where you can move them around, put them in groups and even get rid of them if you need to.

Once you've arranged the sticky notes as you want them, if you stick the big piece of paper on your office wall, then you've always got a changeable, working plan in front of you.

Remember this is YOUR plan to help you achieve YOUR business goals, it needs to be workable and you need to love it. Otherwise there's no point having a plan!

Since I learned about this tip from you I've found it really useful for organising my thoughts.

Sally Smith

BUSINESS TIP NO. 54

Be firm with your prices

A lot of small business owners struggle with setting prices but once you have decided on your prices, stick with them.

There will always be clients/customers who will question your prices but they are your prices not theirs. They might not know your background, experience and knowledge or understand how you got to that value. In my experience, people who try to beat you down on prices are the most difficult to please and are never satisfied. Do you really want customers like that?

Stand your ground and just like your dentist, vet or hairdresser, say this is my 'price' and that is it. You don't need to explain yourself and if you do, it will only make you look desperate.

If they don't like the price, you don't need them and they are certainly not a 'Super Customer'!

Great advice. When I had my Gallery and Framing business, every week there would be at least one customer who would ask "is that your best price" — it took me a long time before I had the confidence to say "yes" to my price and "no" to work I didn't want to do or people I didn't want to work with. I found out the hard way that those Clients/Customers are the hardest to work for and the job you love can soon become the job you hate.

Maggie Hollinshead

I also experienced the fact that clients who want everything for nothing are the hardest to please and to work with.
Knowing your own worth and sticking to your guns is the best thing you can do for your business.

Aga Mortlock

I learnt the hard way at the beginning. Trying to win commissions over sticking to my prices. I wouldn't move on the prices I set now. I know my worth and the hours I put in

Claire Middleton

I really like this tip because we all encounter people who have no idea about the price of our goods and what something unique costs. Everyone is driven by budget prices!!

Julie Austin–Kaye

Totally agree, some times though it's quite normal to second guess yourself, but stick to your guns!

Lesley Lawler

BUSINESS TIP NO. 55

Write a bragging list

I usually talk about this at the year end because it's a good thing to do on those strange days between Christmas and New Year but there's no reason you can't do it at any time of the year. Or even more than once a year.

All you do is go through the past year or months and write down all your business achievements. They can be big, medium or small but they are ALL something that has happened because of you. Because of something you did!

As a nation are not particularly good at blowing our own trumpet or bragging about our achievements. But if we don't write them down how do we know? How can we remember what we have achieved?

I'm sure you'll be surprised about the things you had forgotten.

QUICK WIN

Take a break for 5 minutes and make a list of all the good things that have happened in your business in the past week.

BUSINESS TIP NO. 56

Write down good things that happen

If you already write a gratitude log or a daily journal, you are probably doing this already. But are you doing it specifically for your business?

If something good happens relating to your business, write it down on that day before you forget it. It doesn't matter where you write them but I would write them all in the same place. Or better still, write them on separate pieces of small paper and put them in a jar or a box.

Then you've always got them to look back on, whenever you need to. I find if ever I'm having a bad day (and we all have bad days), getting out my jar and reading through the kind words people have said to me and the good things I have achieved really cheers me up.

They also help with the last business tip 'Write a bragging list'!

From reading this, I have just written some stuff down and will do so going forward. You are right, we certainly have our bad days.

Kerry Burgess

I do this, in my daily gratitude lists. I should definitely write them separately so they're easier to find.

Jennifer Bottrill

BUSINESS TIP NO. 57

You don't have competitors!

I realise that this is a very controversial thing to say! How can we not have competitors?

I am a 100% believer that ALL businesses are unique because as business owners we are ALL different. Therefore if all businesses are different, how can we have competitors?

Being a business owner gets a lot easier when you realise this!

> Stop worrying about what others are doing and use all your energy to building up your unique business.

BUSINESS TIP NO. 58

Create your own luck

I wrote a blog a while ago called 'Do you need luck in business?'. Well the answer, surprisingly is 'Yes you do'!

But the good thing that I've learnt since writing the blog is that we can help create our own good luck.

Put yourself in situations where lucky things can happen. Get out of your comfort zone, go out and meet people, get out of your own way, have a positive attitude...and lots more.

These will all help luck to come your way. Remember to keep your eyes open so you don't miss any opportunities and you will become luckier and more successful.

To improve your luck:
★ Strengthen your talent
★ Focus on where you can make the most difference
★ Work hard to make it happen

BUSINESS TIP NO. 59

Be original

I regularly notice business owners copying other people's ideas and it can be anything from a Facebook post to actual services or products.

Why? Why do they do this?

Because they like something, they see somebody else doing well and think – I'll try that, I'll have some of that. It obviously works for them.

If ever you are tempted...

Well don't, stop it!

You'll never be the same. Remember every business is unique, every business was started by a unique person and their business is unique to them. Their business is successful because they have injected their personality into it.

So no matter how well you copy something it will never be the same, it will never be as good! So why bother? Be yourself, use your own ideas and your own personality and it will shine through.

And if someone copies you (I know, it has happened to me on more than one occasion), no matter how hard it might be at the time, rise above it and take it as a compliment that you're doing so well that people want their own piece of your ACTION. The THING is they can't replicate YOU!!!

BUSINESS TIP NO. 60

In times of uncertainty...

- Don't change what you do
- Remember WHY you are in business
- Adapt your ways of working
- Don't panic!

This came out of one of my Accountability Groups (a group of small business owners who meet monthly to move their businesses forward and I hold them accountable for their actions) but it's relevant for any time you feel uncertainty in your business.

Also remember, we are all in the same boat and need each other. Use whatever resources you have, use each other and if you would like to chat to me, just contact me.

BUSINESS TIP NO. 61

Create a book of awesome

I have to confess that this isn't my idea, it's from Claire Mitchell at 'The Girls mean Business' but it's so wonderful that I need to share it.

Basically it's a place to put all the nice things your clients/customers have said about you. So it's all in one place and when you need to, you can get your book of awesome out and start to read it.

All you do is collect all the nice emails, reviews, recommendations, comments, etc., print them out and stick them in a nice notebook.

Here's Claire explaining what is it and how to use it: https://thegirlsmeanbusiness.com/need–book–awesome–make–one/

I wish I had done this from the beginning. I'm going to start today.

Sue France

I'm going to change the name of my online folder to 'Sally's book of awesomeness;' so much more inspiring than calling it reviews and testimonials!

Sally Smith

BUSINESS TIP NO. 62

Turn threats into opportunities

You've probably heard of SWOT analysis – where you write down your Strengths, Weaknesses, Opportunities and Threats in a table or grid. It's a great exercise to do as a small business owner and one I would repeat annually.

But have you ever thought that a Threat could become an Opportunity?

Threats are something outside your business such as an external trend or change that can reduce your sales or profits and make it hard to achieve your goals, e.g. new technology, competitors or economic changes.

But think about how...
★ New technology can also open new ways for you to do business
★ Loss of customer base is a reason to pursue new customers
★ Economic problems promote fresh ways to promote or sell

It's about looking at the flip side and being open minded. Just think how must more positive it is to have opportunities instead of threats!

BUSINESS TIP NO. 63

Know your numbers

In Business Tip No. 7 I talked about knowing your turnover, gross profit & net profit. But do you know:

1. How much profit you make on each product/service?
2. Which products/services you sell the most?
3. Which products/services make you the most profit?
4. Which product/services make the most money for your business

Knowing these numbers tell you a lot about your business. For instance, there's no point spending a lot of time and money promoting the product/service you sell the most – if it makes you the least profit!

> If you don't know the numbers in your business, then you don't know your business!

BUSINESS TIP NO. 64

Have a website

I can't believe that I've got to Business Tip no. 64 before I mentioned websites!

Having a website for any size or type of business is so important. It gives you credibility, gives you professionalism and you look like a proper business. It's also one of the few marketing tools you actually own.

Personally, I don't tend to buy from anybody without looking at their website first. It tells you so much about a business and about the person/people behind the business.

Also, as one of my clients found out, she doesn't have to keep repeating the answers to the same questions, she just points people to the relevant information on her website.

If you haven't got a website, make sure you get one soon. They don't have to cost a lot of money. With a small amount of technical knowledge you can create your own. The evidence also shows that it can make you feel more business–like.

BUSINESS TIP NO. 65

Know your maximum

number of customers

Are you thinking the answer is – 'as many as I can get'????

Well, that's not the answer! Imagine what would happen if you were over run with customers, if you had more than you would ever need? Could you manage? Could you give them all the same high level of service that you pride yourself in? No you couldn't.

Realistically how many customers/clients can you have?

For instance, say you are a holistic therapist and in order to give each client a high level of service and to allow time for them to come in, have some chit chat, get undressed, have the treatment, get dressed, pay, book another appointment and say goodbye – you like to allow 1.5hrs. If you work 5 days a week from 10am – 6pm and take a 30min break, that means a maximum number of people you can treat in a day is 5 and that's pushing it!

This would be 25 a week, 100 in a month (or 100 sessions).

This number tells you lots of things including:
★ whether you have enough customers?
★ how to set your prices.
★ what's the most money you can earn in a week/month?
★ is it feasible to see this many people or will you be burnt out?

Even Tesco's will know the maximum number of customers they can serve in a day, week, month or even year.

If you don't know yours, work it out now!

This is so true. It is so tempting to help everyone who reaches out for your services but when you give so much attention and energy to each customer, there is a limit to how many you can take on.

Sian-Elin Flint-Freel

Absolutely. My work can often go very deep and I know that to give my best to my clients I can only see a limited number in a day. I'm amazed when I hear hypnotherapists say that they're seeing clients back to back throughout the day. I'm guessing they must just be doing surface suggestion hypnotherapy.

Toni Mackenzie

BUSINESS TIP NO. 66

Look after your customers

There is a great temptation to always be trying to get new customers for your business. But this costs you money and time. Also remember that it's 6/7 times harder to get a new customer/client than to retain the customers you've already got or encourage past customers to come back.

It makes sense that people who have already paid for your products or services like what you are offering and are very important to your business.

Therefore look after them, treat them well, give them more than they expect, make them feel special and show them that they are appreciated.

We are ALL customers/clients to other businesses. Think about how you are treated. What makes you smile if they go above and beyond? This will give you ideas of what works (and what doesn't) when you are looking after and going that extra mile for your own customers/clients.

This is a very good reminder, looking for new clients takes time and money. Be there for your existing ones.

Linda Bretherton

BUSINESS TIP NO. 67

Say who your

customers are

You should know who your 'Super Customers' are (Business Tip No. 20). Those customers/clients who:

★ Love what you do
★ Come back for more
★ Spend Money
★ Don't question your price
★ Recommend & Refer you

So tell other people, on your website, on social media and in your blogs. e.g. I only work with x,y,z.

You might think this is narrowing down your customer base but it's actually saying – "I'm fussy about who I want to work with and I know who I'm looking for." This ensures a good 'fit' between what you are offering and what they want. Because the more Super Customers we can attract the better!

QUICK WIN

In your next social media post, write about what sort of customers/clients you are looking for.

BUSINESS TIP NO. 68

Timing is everything

This business tip is all about seizing opportunities and taking them when the time is right. Carpe Diem!

Look at Zoom – the online meeting software. It was being used in a relatively small way before the Covid–19 pandemic, and most people had never heard of it. Look at it now. Wouldn't it have been nice to have shares in Zoom!

One of my clients, a holistic therapist and yoga teacher, was doing online yoga in a very small way before the pandemic. As soon as lockdown was announced and she realised that she could no longer see clients face to face, she immediately asked her clients if they would like online yoga. The answer was a resounding 'Yes'. She's now doing 9 online classes a week using Zoom!

Note: with both these examples, they where ready, they already knew the concepts worked and when the opportunity came they went for it.

They could have easily sat around and done nothing. Spot when the time is right and take your opportunity!

BUSINESS TIP NO. 69

Change weaknesses

into strengths

Business Tip no. 62 is about SWOT analysis and turning your 'Threats into Opportunities'.

As we all know, nobody is perfect and we all have some weaknesses but what we can do is recognise them, accept them, work with them and use them to our strengths.

For instance, you can ask somebody for help, you can get more prepared, you can hire people with different skills from you or outsource areas of your business or accept that sometimes things don't really matter or 'good is good enough'.

Using your weaknesses in the right ways will help you to become stronger and therefore a better business owner.

BUSINESS TIP NO. 70

Do what people will

pay for

We've all seen people set up a business with an amazing idea or something they love to do and then struggle to sell or grow the business.

Your idea might be the most fantastic in the world and you might be the world's best at doing something but is it actually a business?

Will people pay their hard earned cash for it? If not, you don't have a business.

Just because you'd pay for it, doesn't mean others will.

BUSINESS TIP NO. 71

Sell what people want not what they need

Following on from Business Tip No. 70 – 'Do what people will pay for', you also need to sell what people want, not what they need.

We all need things in order to live, feed, clothe ourselves, travel, etc but what makes us want something?

Expensive designer brands sell wants all the time. I don't need that very expensive Chanel bag but I want it! I want it in my life for lots of reasons.

For your product or service, firstly identify that there is a need and secondly, that people want it. Particularly if your product/service satisfies a want that is currently not being met or not being met very well.

Satisfying wants will make people return to your business again and again!

Ooo that's interesting. I've noticed that sometimes clients approach me with what they want but we discover together it is not what they need. However, to come to me in the first place they need to be attracted to me providing what they want.

Sian-Elin Flint-Freel

BUSINESS TIP NO. 72

Sell benefits

In the last two business tips we learnt that we need to sell what people will pay for and also sell want they want. Another tip is selling benefits.

Talk about the benefits of your product/service all the time. People do need to know about the features of your product but what they really want to know is:

★ what am I going to gain?
★ how am I going to feel?
★ how will this help me?
★ what's in it for me?

Take Search Engine Optimisation; most people don't understand it, think it's very technical and will switch off during a conversation about it. But what they want to know is: Will it get me more clients? Will it get me on the first page of a Google search? Will my right customers/clients be able to find me easily? etc.

It's tempting to talk about how hard you work, how much money you have invested in the product, etc. but harsh though it is, people just aren't interested!

Good advice. Sometimes we have to be harsh to be clear.

Linda Bretherton

Great advice - meet people where they are with information about what's important to them.

Sally Smith

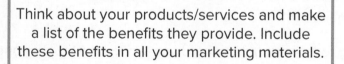

QUICK WIN

Think about your products/services and make a list of the benefits they provide. Include these benefits in all your marketing materials.

BUSINESS TIP NO. 73

Show your worth

Your product/service is only worth what your customers **think** it is worth. They need to see the value in what you are offering before they will buy.

So how do you show your worth or value to them? Not easy questions to answer!

A good start is to follow the last three business tips:

1. Do what people will pay for
2. Sell want people want not what they need
3. Sell benefits

If your product/service is something people will pay for, if they want it and they can see the benefits they will get. Then they will see the value and its worth.

These 3 things add up to the value. They need to see the value, then they will buy. Simples!

Results from happy clients are an excellent way to show your worth - even better when they say it for you!
Sian-Elin Flint-Freel

BUSINESS TIP NO. 74

Know how much money

you need a month

You may think this is irrelevant, as don't we all want to make as much money as possible each month? Well, yes we do but if we know we need to make £2k each month to pay our bills and we are only making £1k, then something is seriously wrong.

I'm always surprised by how little some clients know about money. About how much they need and how much they need to make.

So if you don't know how much money you need each month, then work it out now. As every penny over this amount is extra spends for you!!

BUSINESS TIP NO. 75

Read - Listen - Watch

Have an open mindset and expand your horizons. Search around your subject and area of expertise.

Read books, magazines, newspapers. Listen to podcasts or audiobooks. Watch videos.

You will always find something of interest to expand your knowledge and learn from.

There's a big world of information out there that's easy to access. Make the most of it!

For me, ongoing professional development is also ongoing personal development and I'll never stop learning and growing...

Toni Mackenzie

BUSINESS TIP NO. 76

Update your skills

One thing is sure in life and business and that is nothing stays the same. The world is continuously evolving and so our expertise, skills and knowledge should too.

Some ways to update your skills might be obvious, such as industry relevant training courses. But there's lots of other ways like reading books, industry conferences, connecting with leaders in your industry or joining an association.

And don't forget to practise your newly learned skills!

QUICK WIN

Choose one thing you can easily do to improve your skill in an area of your business.

BUSINESS TIP NO. 77

Keep learning

If you are not a life-long learner, become one now! From a business point of view, learn around your subject, read and follow people who inspire you, watch business programmes and look at everything with fresh eyes.

Some of the many benefits to learning are:
1. Renewed self–motivation
2. Recognition of personal interests and goals
3. Improvement in other personal and professional skills
4. Improved self–confidence
           ... and enjoyment!

Never stop learning. It's great to be open to new ideas, be aware of what's happening in your own area or industry but also, I think, to challenge yourself to stay alert, fresh and interesting/interested.

Maggie Hollinshead

I'm a big fan of self improvement. Taking the time to renew whilst picking up handy hints and tips.

Sally Prescott

BUSINESS TIP NO. 78

Unfollow bad influencers

Do you ever find yourself reading or listening to somebody (particularly on social media) and thinking...

...this really isn't making me feel good?
...I don't like what they are saying?

Then STOP and UNFOLLOW them!

Life is too short to waste our time with people who make us feel bad!

I definitely agree that people have a different impact on you as time goes on and you have to stay tuned to how it makes you feel and do something about it.

Caroline Cubbon

BUSINESS TIP NO. 79

Be a Cheerleader

Let's face it, being a business owner isn't easy at times and we all need a little extra help or to feel appreciated. So let's vow to help each other and spread the word about our fellow business owners as much as we can.

Every small thing you do will help, such as:

★ Interacting on social media – like, comment and share posts
★ Writing recommendations
★ Referring them to people who would benefit from their skills and expertise

Essential that we support others and do what we can to put a spring in their business step.

Caroline Cubbon

BUSINESS TIP NO. 80

Connect people together

Do you ever meet somebody and a light bulb goes off in your head? You think this person needs to talk to so and so.....they'll be great for each other, they have so much in common or they can help each other in business?

I know a lot of business owners, so this happens to me all the time and I make sure I connect the two people together.

I've also had it happen to me, where somebody has put me in contact with somebody else. This is wonderful and makes my day.

So next time you think two people should be connected, make sure you go ahead and connect them.

You never know where it might lead for either of them!

BUSINESS TIP NO. 81

Support groups you like

If you have social media or networking groups that you like, then support them as much as you can.

This can be by:
* attending events
* recommending them to other business owners
* giving raffle prizes
* offering to help set up the room or with refreshments
* having a stall at events

Remember, we can all do with a little extra help and support at times.

Absolutely! If we can't support each other, what can we do?
Lisa Harper

Totally! I've met some wonderful people, and some great customers too through groups. These are the people who 'get' that it's more than just my business, and cheer me on whenever I least expect it!
Samantha Robson

BUSINESS TIP NO. 82

Networking is not

about selling

If you go to networking events with the objective of selling, then you will fail!

Nobody wants to be obviously sold to by somebody who only talks about their business or thrusts a business card in your face as soon as you meet them. If you do this, they will run away as fast as possible.

This is what gives networking events a bad name.

Take it easy, chill, get to know people. Talk about the weather or the journey or whatever. Find out if you genuinely have things in common by asking them questions that will help them talk about themselves, their hopes and dreams. Networking is about building relationships.

This is so true. I've been to quite a few where people have done exactly that and haven't asked one question about me. It instantly puts you off!

Zoë Oughton

Oh goodness, I couldn't agree more. No one likes to be sold to. Be interested in people - as humans - and let the relationships grow.

Catherine Sandland

I totally agree with this! I've never tried to 'sell' at networking events. I feel that by just going with the flow and having natural conversations with whoever you happen to meet you are authentically 'selling' yourself.

Toni Mackenzie

BUSINESS TIP NO. 83

Follow up on connections

How many times do you:

* chat to somebody about business
* meet somebody at a networking event
* swap business cards with somebody

and then never hear from them again?

Sales people used to say 'Fortune is in the followup' – and I don't mean selling!

Connect to people afterwards, say 'Hello', ask how they are getting on, show interest, start following them on social media.

You are building up your networks and you never know something might lead from that initial connection.

Following up after making new connections through networking is the most important part. There is no point in spending time and money networking if we don't follow up by way of a one to one coffee or even an email or phone call and certainly LinkedIn.

Tricia Peters

BUSINESS TIP NO. 84

Recognise weak connections

A weak connection or a weak tie is:

* ★ an acquaintance
* ★ another business owner you exchanged a business card with
* ★ somebody you speak to only when you see them at networking events
* ★ social media followers
* ★ somebody you vaguely know

These connections are very valuable to us because they are people we don't know very well. We are not likely to be in touch with them very often and don't necessarily mix in the same circles.

There is a theory that weak connections are likely to be more influential than close friends, particularly in social networks, because they will have large networks of their own, most of which you do not know. So if someone who is a weak connection talks to their friends and networks about you, you are being introduced to a whole network of people who you have never met.

So recognise them, strengthen them, become a connector and expand your network!

Weak connections always work best for me. You are one good example, Karen. Our relationship started by knowing each other briefly in networking groups. In time, you can build up the relationship and it leads you to new ones.

Senem Peace

Someone I got to know via networking became a client (actually for her daughter), I then became her client, she referred a dream client to me, this dream client has sent me her friends. It's a ripple effect, isn't it? And that's why we love networking.

Yifan Nairn

BUSINESS TIP NO. 85

There's only 10 months in a business year

This doesn't mean that you are only running your business 10 months of the year.

What is does mean is:
* you WILL take holidays
* you might be sick
* August might be quiet
* Christmas might be quiet for at least 2 weeks (or as I find, more like 4 weeks!)

Unless you sell products online, you are not available 52 weeks of the year!

Therefore, if you are doing any forward projection calculations on your business, such as 'What's the maximum number of appointments?' or 'How much profit I can have in a year?', then it's easier and more realistic to work on 10 months.

Definitely worth being realistic about downtime, contingency time and the true amount of productive working time in any given week, month and year. It's easy to fall into the trap of getting those basics wrong then feel as though you are constantly lagging behind.

Caroline Cubbon

BUSINESS TIP NO. 86

Know your boundaries

Lots of people talk about business owners setting boundaries because they are very important. When I worked in an office 9–5, 5 days a week, I very rarely worked outside of those hours. I left the work – at the office.

When you work for yourself the temptation is that you are always available 24/7, you can always be contacted, you never switch off.

Unless you operate an emergency service, there is simply no need to be always available. It is bad for you and bad for your business which makes it bad for your customers

We need to switch off, take a break, take a holiday, have a work/life balance.

When we are well rested everybody – you, your family and your customers – all benefit.

Set your boundaries, know what they are and very importantly, make sure your communicate them to your clients/customers.

That's so true and so important! I have to remind myself of this constantly, I always want to answer messages straight away.

Zoë Oughton

Really good point and something I struggle with. I make myself too available and am always on duty as a result. Having boundaries helps to manage expectations and encourages people to respect your time more too.

Caroline King

This is so important. I've just started my business and I've been working 24/7. Need to get boundaries set early doors!

Sophie Birley–Brown

BUSINESS TIP NO. 87

Don't be a busy fool

I have a client who wants to meet me to help her focus on growing her business. We make an appointment, she cancels it because she says she's 'too busy', we then make another appointment, she cancels it because she's 'too busy'.

Can you see the problem here?

She won't spend an hour with me sorting out her busyness because she's too busy!

It's much easier for her to stay in her comfort zone being busy but not being effective. Rather than fixing the problem once and for all.

She's being a busy fool. If this is you, don't be a busy fool!

QUICK WIN

Pick the task you've being putting off the most and do it now!

BUSINESS TIP NO. 88

Have services/products

at different levels

This is about what's known as 'Pyramid Pricing'. Think about a pyramid with different levels.

At the bottom is the widest level, this is for the majority of people and is usually your cheapest or free products. So it's your website, social media, newsletters, freebies, etc.

The second level is your introductory products, it's for a smaller number of people than the bottom level and it's an entry point for you to get new paying clients/customers. It may be an offer or something at a low price to attract people to your business.

The third level is for even an even smaller number of people, it's probably for clients/customers to purchase your average priced products/services.

You can have as many levels as you need but the top of the pyramid is the crème de la crème, the pièce de résistance for VIP clients only. It's for very few clients/customers and it's your most expensive product.

Clients can start at the bottom of the pyramid and work their way up or they can go straight to the top or somewhere in the middle. It doesn't matter but what does matter is that you have various levels for different people at different prices. Because not everybody's needs are the same and not everybody wants or can afford to be your VIP client.

Remember not everybody is willing to take a chance on you (why should they?). Let them build up trust and confidence in you at the lower levels before they plunge for your most expensive service or product.

QUICK WIN

Draw yourself a triangle with levels inside and write your products/services in each one.

BUSINESS TIP NO. 89

Give away your knowledge

Basically, don't hold on to knowledge, share it.....

In today's world, fewer and fewer people will pay for knowledge, everywhere it is given away for free, for example on websites, YouTube and social media. People won't pay for you to teach them how to do something if they can find a YouTube video which explains the same thing.

So give it away, on your website, in your social media posts, in newsletters, freebies, etc.

The advantage is that people get to know you, understand where you are coming from, know how you go about things. It starts them on the 'know–like–trust' journey with you.

BUSINESS TIP NO. 90

Begin with the end in mind

This isn't my quote, it's habit no. 2 in Stephen Covey's book, 'The 7 habits of highly effective people'. If you haven't read the book, I can highly recommend it.

It's all about visualising how you want something to look like, to feel like, to smell like, etc. in the future. Then figuring out how to make it happen.

It's a very powerful tool.

I use it with my clients for goal setting. I ask them to think about 12 months in the future: What do you want your business to look like? What do you want to be doing? We then use this vision to work backwards to write our SMART goal and plan step by step how to get there.

I did this when deciding what to do next in Autumn 2016 as I didn't want to put retired after recovering from a serious illness. I was renewing my passport and had to put something down as occupation. I put artist down even though I hadn't picked up a pencil or paint brush at that point. And look what I've achieved so far in this capacity.

Louise Barson

BUSINESS TIP NO. 91

Nothing is cast in stone

As business owners we are in charge of our own destiny, we set the rules, we decide how we want our business to run.

Therefore, if its no longer working for you, in any shape or form, then change it.

Nothing is so permanent it is cast in stone!

Absolutely, if it's not working change the business formula. Done that a few times.

Kerry Louise Burgess

BUSINESS TIP NO. 92

Your business will evolve

Don't expect to be running your business in exactly the same way in year 3 or year 5 or year 10 as you was in year 1. Because you won't be and that's good.

Over time, we change, our ideas change and so do our customers.

Evolve your business – it's a good thing to do and keeps it and you fresh.

BUSINESS TIP NO. 93

It takes time

When I started my business an accountant said to me: "It will take 3 years before you feel like you are getting somewhere, 4 years before you are getting somewhere and 5 years before you are there".

I thought: 'Really? That's a long time!' But you know, it's true and I've met lots of other business owners who all say the same thing. It all takes a long time to get your business to where you want it to be.

Remember you are in this for the long haul. But it's well worth it.

Yes, can vouch for that. Ten years and I still need to be on the ball.
Nicky Abell-Francis

Year 18 and still not there - always improving. Still enjoying it. It's like a roller coaster, scary at first, but thrilling.
Gaynor Sinar

Great reminder. No overnight wins running your own business.
Kirsty James

BUSINESS TIP NO. 94

Outsourcing is good

I'm often asked by clients – 'Should I outsource?' and my answer is that there are two reasons why you should outsource:

1. If you are too busy doing the actual business to have time to do your admin, accounts, etc.

or

2. If you absolutely hate doing the admin, accounts, etc.

Then you are better paying somebody to do these jobs, so you can spend your time doing what you really 'love' to do and getting paid for it!

Absolutely! I've just began to unlock the control and outsource.
Julie Widdowson

If I didn't outsource, I don't think our children's picture books would look very good. Stick figures don't really do a story justice!
Sue Miller

BUSINESS TIP NO. 95

Listen

When you were a child, did your parents say to you: 'You have **two ears** and **one mouth** so that you can listen twice as much as you speak'?

This relates very well to business...

The more **you listen**, the more people will **talk**. The more they feel heard, the more they will trust and like **you**. Keep them **talking** and keep **listening**. If they like **you** and trust **you**, **you** are more likely to make the sale.

So use your ears twice as much as your mouth and listen...to clients/ customers, suppliers, employees. In fact, everybody!

I so agree. Who do we avoid at networking events? The person who only talks about themselves and tries to monopolise the conversation. We never buy from them.
Sue France

Never a truer word. In the words of Covey: 'Seek first to understand'. Rather than listening to reply. My clients want to learn about them, not me. Then, by me listening, they learn about me.

Linzi Wood

It's so important to listen to someone else as what they say may point you in a new direction of opportunities!

Anne Moore

BUSINESS TIP NO. 96

No doesn't always

mean never!

I listened to a podcast with Kanya King, who is the CEO and founder of the MOBO organisation. The podcast was full of lots of fantastic insights for business owners and a few brilliant snippets.

One of them was – 'NO' stands for 'NOT OVER'. As business owners we have to get used to rejection and hearing the word 'No'. Kanya says it's 'not over' as there is always a possibility they might say 'Yes'!

I've heard this idea before but I definitely believe that 'No' can mean 'No' and there's no point pushing and pursuing somebody if they are really not interested. That's not good for you or your business.

But I do believe that if people are genuinely interested in your business and they say 'No', it probably means that it's a 'No' for now but sometime in the future (for lots of reasons!) it could be a 'Yes'!

True. I have now worked with people who said no to me years ago.
Sue France

Great point. Readiness for change is not always immediate.
Linzi Wood

BUSINESS TIP NO. 97

Ensure your customers/clients

are a good fit

If you meet your customers/clients more than once then you want to ensure that they are a good fit for you and your business. Are you going to get on? Do you both want the same outcomes from your working relationship? Are you what they are looking for? Are they the right customer for you?

My suggestion is to meet them or speak to them before you actually start working together. Most coaches do this by giving 'discovery calls'.

If you don't think you are going to be a 'good' fit, then tell them. I'm sure they will appreciate the honesty.

At the end of the day, not everybody is your customer and a 'bad fit' customer will only cause you problems in the future.

So many of my clients think I can pull out of thin air their thoughts on a holiday. If they won't have a consultation I won't do the quote! It's a big purchase and if they are serious they will make an appointment. I get many time wasters in my profession. Some people's hobby is just getting quotes!

Laura Featonby

BUSINESS TIP NO. 98

Two strikes and you're out!

Do you ever have customers/clients who mess you about? Don't answer emails or messages, don't pay on time, etc?

I do, we all do. But we don't need it and basically, if they are not keen and committed, then they are not your customer.

So give them two chances and then move on and forget them.

(Hopefully you are getting paid upfront, so if they don't pay then you haven't lost anything!)

BUSINESS TIP NO. 99

Beware of continuous discounting

Do you often have discounts on your products or services?

Do you have more than 1 discount on at once?

Is this a good idea?

I remember a very well-known high street clothes retailer who always had a sale on. They probably didn't but it seemed that way as a customer.

What happened was I would have a look around the shop and if I found something that I wanted to buy I would simply wait until the sale was on. What was the point of paying full price when you knew that in a few weeks it would be reduced?

The consequence of this was that they never sold at full price!

So if you regularly discount in your business, think...

How does this appear to your customers? What will they think?

It can look confusing but it can also look a bit desperate. If your prices are correct and you are confident in them, people will see the value and pay the full price!

BUSINESS TIP NO. 100

Word of the year

Have you set a 'word of the year' for yourself or do you intend to?

Having a word of the year is a really good thing to do at the start of a new year, to set your intention and theme for the year ahead. It's not as rigid as setting goals but is an easy way to guide the next 12 months.

When you need to make a decision or something happens, think – does this fit with my word? If it doesn't, you have answered the question.

If you are not sure how to come up with your 'word' (and I definitely struggle with it), try these steps:

1. On a piece of paper, make two columns. On one side, write down everything that went well over the past year. On the other side, write what you would like to change.

2. Review the list of what went well. How do these things make you feel? What do you want more of?

3. Choose one to five words that really speak to how you want your year to feel. Nouns, verbs, anything works—just words that feel good to you. Don't get caught up in the grammar.

4. Review the words, then narrow it down to one that you know in your heart you need more of.

5. Then write your word somewhere where you will see it every day.

I've ended up with TIME
Do I have time to say yes, take on more?
Do I value what's taking time? Structure to save time
Have I made time for family and friends?
Have I made time for me?
Thanks Karen. I love it!

Hayley Brown

Gut! A couple of times last year I should have listened to my gut feeling, I think it's always right.

Nicola Henshaw

Mine is Self—belief. I need to trust myself more.

Becky Field

QUICK WIN

You don't have to always set your 'Word of the Year' at the beginning of each year. If you haven't got one for this year, do the quick exercise of setting one now!

BUSINESS TIP NO. 101

Don't bet the farm

I've left this one till last, as it's so important. As a business owner you have total autonomy over how you run your business. You can take risks, try new things, push the boundaries. But there is one thing you must never, never do and that is – don't bet the farm.

Basically business is about taking considered risks NOT gambling. So don't risk anything you can't afford to lose and therefore end up with nothing.

THANK YOU

I'd like to give huge thanks to the following people, who without their vision and insight, this book would not have been created.

Sue France – for having the initial idea, believing in me at the beginning and her constant support.

Siân-Elin Flint-Freel – book mentor, copyeditor and proofreader extraordinaire for her incredible level of detail and always knowing what's right!

Caroline Cubbon – my communications expert friend for giving her positive critical eye in approving the layout as a pre–reader.

To the numerous business owners whose comments on the business tips have given the book more depth and reality.

And last but not least to Tony, my long suffering partner, who has the patience of a saint and is always there as my rock of encouragement.

238

ABOUT THE AUTHOR

Karen Taylor has over 30 years' experience as a business 'trouble shooter' and now works as a Business Mentor and Website Creator for small local businesses. She is a strong advocate of supporting local independent businesses and encouraging others to think about where they spend their money. She lives in Cheshire, UK with her partner, Tony and enjoys walking their dog, Bob, yoga and macramé.

HOW TO CONTACT KAREN

I would love to hear from you if you have found the Business Tips in this book useful and how they have helped your business. You will find my contact details on any of the links below:

https://karenyourbusinessmentor.com
https://karenyourwebsitecreator.com
https://www.facebook.com/karenyourbusinessmentor
https://www.instagram.com/karenyourbusinessmentor/

If you have enjoyed and benefited from this book, I would appreciate you leaving a review of the book on the platform where you bought the book.

Thank you.

Lightning Source UK Ltd.
Milton Keynes UK
UKHW052144291021
393073UK00004B/36